WHITE DECIMAL

WHITE DECIMAL   JEAN DAIVE

 translated by   NORMA COLE

OMNIDAWN PUBLISHING
OAKLAND, CALIFORNIA
2017

Cover art by Ajit Chauhan: *Forty Miles Apart,*
typewriter ink, pencil on paper 11 3/4 x 8 1/4 inches.
Courtesy of the artist.

Cover and interior fonts: Adobe Garamond 3 LT Std and Kabel LT Std

Cover and interior design by Gillian Olivia Blythe Hamel

Offset printed in the United States
by Edwards Brothers Malloy, Ann Arbor, Michigan
On 55# Enviro Natural 100% Recycled 100% PCW
Acid Free Archival Quality FSC Certified Paper

Library of Congress Cataloging-in-Publication Data

Names: Daive, Jean, author. | Cole, Norma, translator. | Daive, Jean. Poems.
  Selections. English. | Daive, Jean. Poems. Selections.
Title: White decimal / Jean Daive ; translated by Norma Cole.
Description: Oakland, California : Omnidawn Publishing, 2017. | Bilingual
  edition (English and French). Originally published in French as: Dâecimale
  blanche.
Identifiers: LCCN 2017022802 | ISBN 9781632430489 (pbk. : alk. paper)
Classification: LCC PQ2664.A46 A2 2017 | DDC 841/.914--dc23
LC record available at https://lccn.loc.gov/2017022802

Published by Omnidawn Publishing, Oakland, California
www.omnidawn.com   (510) 237-5472   (800) 792-4957
10 9 8 7 6 5 4 3 2 1
ISBN: 978-1-63243-048-9

CONTENTS

WHITE DECIMAL

white decimal

at the edge of space

I wandered
between refusal and insistence
looking on the ground

snowing
name unmakes form
the thaw the avalanche
                    remakes absence

separated
    for ever   visible   exposed

exempt

porous

in silence
in sickness

    and possessing the gift of breath
            the gift of healing

while I followed time
        to rise toward the attribute

the initiate
in the separation
rethinks all knowledge

the dead
sinks into nothingness
in the circle of all the attitudes
and seeks to defer
the state of incompletion

nothing but my body
and what is external to
the physical movement of my fall

      the beams of emptiness
dividing the stays, the hearths, the spheres

    the labyrinth
of an incomplete attitude
is the thread of all labyrinths

            its transfiguration
                on the inside of death

silent as the embrace

the pivotal voice

where one of the shades is declared C.

now
time erases the mortal fable

the old woman far away threw my voice

unearth she says
unearth

       it is snowing
              beneath the bowl
              is snowing body of the peak

the old woman is four times

the race was waiting for one of the shades
and wanted to call him C.

one of one appeared
and C. was his name

I was suddenly that fire before her
                        already the race
                        beyond ash
                        kneeling in the cold

I walk to begin

illuminated from below through death
was I ever whiteness

I heard weeping from the neighboring race
                                    I hear
unearth   unearth

I hear the man
in his solitude
telling himself stories of dragons

she says
white is not dividing four grey by
zero but dividing their decimals by zero

time hides itself
and I stir through the flame

the bowl is empty
where she drank with the race

it is said that transparency comes from above
hers came from salt

   appeared
in the light of the four decimals of the name

   seen   called   in spite of

then
the blue the blue and the descent in the spiral of her name
by the counterweight of the scream

I called I called C.
oh the alternation of blue and white in time

then

at the exit of absence
like a peal of laughter denying the embrace
the old woman

who is twice C. once me once

mother

mother mother and me

alone
nothing in himself
closed

it was the moment
it was he watching himself pass

white insect resting in death

and the moment is the water surprised between the lock and the ark distances embraces

        nothing but the bowl
and again

            boundless
                snow
above the thirst opening on myth

in the beginning
I was four times

then I buried my sex
to live in crystal

she disappeared
under cover of snow
to serve as ground to emptiness

who embodies its name becomes decimal
she said

she said
I sought the name for whom the spoken chain
orders the world
animates forces silences speech
and owns the whiteness
of refusal and insistence

I heard her weeping in the race

who knows to what she yields
when she follows and exceeds it

it matters no more that the sea is green
since blue no longer makes us ill
she said

(she is more blue than the sea)

she is winter
    white
    the black dot in the storm
    low on the horizon

(yet the snow did not make her white)

she is at the heart of eternity
        the whiteness of the moment

gap o vault
what obscure expert knowledge
does not seize the stunned one
on the flight path

what spot loses her
what point finds her

o line
what gap recognizes its angle
what scream creates the abyss in her voice

she calls she calls she rests

now that the scream has spent her voice her speech

she flies high up in the sky
reveals to me the shores the blue the stain

she is what seems to never end

blue her face
but reaching back behind
the water of her eyes

she speaks she lies she simplifies

gap of no surface
image of no face
she enters in silence
covers the polygon of death

she keeps watch over the attitude of the line
and the wrinkle comes to stay on her face

power of the first division

    of the sod of the earth
announcing the entrance of the initiate into death

form of presences
physical form of beginnings

the initial
opens the book the pursuit of the labyrinth
torture
of gestures of words of attitudes
denouncing the transforming proportion
        of the shade in its shade

      the red matter of its space

blades of transparent earth
crepuscular
heights
that subterranean denials
double
  and the eye that remains in the dust

past
inexhaustibly
at the edge of the visible

white
of a light
homeless aimless

breath following the memory of differences
space becomes mental
              blindfold
on its horizon
torn
within
the gulf in the abyss

and I leave my gaze on her gaze
behind her countenance
after this world

              the void
the void
the abstract void precedes me into death

.

near possible
something a sign
like an utterance
such white saliva

the simple appearance
            in spite of the matter of the name
coming out of silence
            of the cold

lost in the contemplation of her end
denial separates from her

and beginning in the beginning
the water that dreams her
and disposes of her in the invisible maze
seeks the smooth perfection of the sea

on the grounds (the sojourns)
where a dark device floods
glides water linen
that changes knowledge
into elemental wreck

at the bottom of the stairs
where the spiral lasts an instant
hesitates
stuns the step

it is the moment
fearsome whiteness

that time never recaptures

time describes a circle in space

and space inside begins
other circles larger
other times longer

no resemblance returns toward self nor toward god
no image
no silence

only the last one instructs the spheres
and contains all beginning

he substitutes space for furniture
that contains all the light
he opens its infinite drawers
dwells in them
closes them
and climbs climbs up
to the closed room
where the sky seeks its stars
and the moon its tides

he considers
the harness lost inland
prolonging snow
the furrows
the black rays of the sun

things beings running toward the same white dot

he considers
the universe immobilizing a phrase
(which is algebra to him the letters)
that silence spells simplifies
that voice declares repeats

repeats
for the simple sums give the surface
and double sums motion

four is the attribute of C.

before
when laughter bore the embrace
when blue afflicted the slate and the sea

he went back up the hill
he went back up the avalanche
where the summits meet

with his insect voice
and his broad countenance

the boundless gesture
the taut scarf

the comb is the last degree of gesture
and I am the one who falls
who is added and is added no more
place of staying and place of knowing

named
and at once in spite of myself
felt

in the counter-day of death

I rise from the depth of my likeness
to the limit of the enigma

evening after evening
I disappeared I am disappearing

she is dazzled
she falls into the fabric of cold

sometimes the return
(is it haste)
relieves the lingering

                        that delays in his midst
speech
to represent absence

the thread
while it divulges the fable of life

among the imaginary weft

the other reveals
the eternal weaver

immense arch over the sea
where the back bends
or the gesture lifts up the avalanche
while the shoulder gives way

she was reading something about the quantum leap
she was reading
                without knowing
that she completes what the lamp and the window begins

among the three glimmers

pure lamp of no book

far
as appearing

the white voice
what stiff pensive line
alluding to what is no longer the roof the hall

        very pure

the tree erases water and begins again

I enter and leave
and seek what opens and closes again

I saw evanesce in the wind
the last glimmer of the last evening
in the drawing out of the light

then the wing was slower
and the angle wider

crossing the sky
the stain unfurled the tree the water

from the other side
not a leaf

dreaming the slow geometry
of tile and slate

as theorem
at the discovery of what is the roof the hall

she speaks she renews her chasms

she says
absent
she was one of the three glimmers
resting in spite of the cold
far from the window and the lamp

she says
she haunted what absence no longer holds
the glimmer
that held it before her
she felt from it a moment of unknown pain
at absolving the lamp and the window

DÉCIMALE BLANCHE

décimale blanche

au bord de l'espace

j'ai erré
entre refus et insistance
regardant par la terre

neiger
le nom défaire la forme
la fonte l'avalanche
                    refaire l'absence

séparé
    à jamais   apparent   découvert

franchi

poreux

dans le silence
dans la maladie

    et possédant le don du souffle
                le don de guérison

tandis que je longeais l'heure
             pour remonter vers l'attribut

(l'initié
dans la séparation
repense tous les savoirs

le mort
s'enfonce dans l'anéantissement
dans le cercle de toutes les attitudes
et cherche à éloigner
l'état d'inachèvement

rien que mon corps
et ce qui est extérieur
au mouvement physique de ma chute

    les faisceaux du vide
divisant les séjours les foyers les globes

    le labyrinthe
d'une attitude inachevée
est le fil de tous les labyrinthes

        sa transfiguration
          à l'intérieur de la mort)

silencieuse comme l'étreinte

la voix pivotale

où un de l'ombre se prononce C.

maintenant
l'heure efface la fable mortelle

la vieille femme au loin lança ma voix

déterre dit-elle
déterre

    il neige
       au-dessous du bol
       neige corps du sommet

la vieille femme est quatre fois

la race attendait un de l'ombre
et voulait l'appeler C.

un de un apparut
et C. fut son nom

je fus soudain ce feu en avant d'elle
        déjà la race
    au delà de la cendre
    à genoux dans le froid

je marche pour me commencer

éclairé d'en bas à travers la mort
fus-je jamais blancheur

j'ai entendu pleurer dans la race voisine
                                    j'entends
déterre   déterre

j'entends l'homme
dans sa solitude
se raconter des histoires de dragons

elle dit
le blanc n'est pas la division de quatre gris par
zéro mais la division de leurs décimales par zéro

l'heure se couvre
et je vibre à travers la flamme

' le bol est vide
où elle but avec la race

il est dit que la transparence vient du haut
la sienne venait du sel

   apparut
à la lumière des quatre décimales du nom

   vu   appelé   malgré

puis
le bleu le bleu et la descente dans la spirale du nom
par le contrepoids du cri

j'ai appelé j'ai appelé C.
oh l'alternance du bleu et du blanc dans l'heure

puis

.

au sortir de l'absence
comme un éclat de rire niant l'étreinte
la vieille femme

qui est deux fois C. une fois moi une fois

mère

mère mère et moi

seul
nul en lui-même
clos

il fut l'instant
il fut qui se regarde passer

insecte blanc posé dans la mort

et l'instant est l'eau surprise entre l'écluse et l'arche

des distances des étreintes

rien que le bol
et de nouveau

immense
la neige
au-dessus de la soif ouvrant sur le mythe

au commencement
je fus quatre fois

puis j'enterrai mon sexe
pour vivre dans le cristal

elle disparut
à la faveur de la neige
pour tenir lieu de fond au vide

qui incarne son nom devient décimale
dit-elle

elle dit
j'ai cherché le nom dont la chaîne parlée
ordonne le monde
anime les forces les silences la parole
et possède la blancheur
du refus et de l'insistance

je l'ai entendue pleurer dans sa race

nul ne sait à quoi elle cède
lorsqu'elle le suit et qu'elle le dépasse

il n'importe plus que la mer soit verte
puisque le bleu ne nous fait plus mal
dit-elle

(elle est le bleu en plus de la mer)

elle est l'hiver
    blanc
    le point noir de l'orage
    au bas de l'horizon

(pourtant la neige ne la fit pas blanche)

elle est au coeur de l'éternel
      la blancheur de l'instant

écart ô voûte
quelle science obscure de l'avertie
ne détienne celle de l'étonnée
dans le trajet d'une ligne

quel lieu la perd
quel point la retrouve

ô ligne
quel écart reconnaît son angle
quel cri fait l'abîme dans la voix

elle appelle elle appelle elle repose

maintenant que le cri a dépensé la voix la parole

elle passe très haut dans le ciel
et m'en révèle les bords le bleu la tache

elle est ce qui semble ne jamais finir

bleu le visage
mais passant très loin derrière
l'eau des yeux

elle parle elle ment elle se simplifie

écart d'aucune aire
image d'aucune figure
elle entre dans le silence
couvre le polygone de mort

elle veille dans l'attitude de la ligne
et la ride est le séjour de son visage

pouvoir de la première division

      de la motte de terre
annonçant l'entrée de l'initié dans la mort

formule des présences
formule physique des commencements

l'initiale
ouvre le livre la poursuite du labyrinthe
le supplice
des gestes des mots des attitudes
dénonçant la transformante proportion
      de l'ombre dans son ombre

      la matière rouge de son espace

lames de la terre transparente
hauteurs
crépusculaires
que les négations souterraines
dédoublent
        et l'œil qui se tient dans la poussière

passé
inépuisablement
au bord du visible

blanc
d'une lumière
sans foyer sans objet

le souffle succédant à la mémoire des différences
l'espace devient mental
                    bandeau
sur son horizon
déchiré
à l'intérieur
du gouffre dans l'abîme

et je laisse mon regard sur son regard
derrière son visage
après ce monde

                    le vide
le vide
le vide abstrait me précède dans la mort

proche possible
quelque chose un signe
comme un énoncé
une salive très blanche

l'apparence simple
        malgré la matière du nom
au sortir du silence
        du froid

perdue dans la contemplation de sa fin
la négation se détache d'elle-même

et commencement dans le commencement
l'eau qui la rêve
et la dispose dans le dédale de l'invisible
cherche la lisse perfection de la mer

sur les sols (les séjours)
qu'un obscur appareil inonde
glisse un linge d'eau
qui métamorphose le savoir
en loque élémentale

au bas de l'escalier
où la spirale dure un moment
hésite
étourdit la marche

il est l'instant
effrayant de blancheur

que l'heure jamais ne reprend

l'heure décrit un cercle dans l'espace

et l'espace à l'intérieur commence
d'autres cercles plus larges
d'autres heures plus longues

nulle ressemblance ne renvoie vers soi ni vers dieu
nulle image
nul silence

seulement le dernier instruit les sphères
et contient tout commencement

il substitue l'espace à un meuble
qui contient toute la lumière
il en ouvre les tiroirs infinis
les habite
les ferme
et monte monte
jusqu'à la chambre close
où le ciel cherche ses astres
et la lune ses marées

il regarde
l'attelage perdu dans les terres
prolonger la neige
les sillons
les rayons noirs du soleil

les choses les êtres courir vers un même point blanc

il   regarde
l'univers immobiliser une phrase
(elle en est l'algèbre lui les lettres)
que le silence épelle simplifie
que la voix dénonce répète

répète
puisque les sommes simples donnent la surface
et les sommes doubles le mouvement

quatre est l'attribut de C.

autrefois
quand le rire portait l'étreinte
quand le bleu désolait l'ardoise et la mer

il remontait la colline
il remontait l'avalanche
où se mêlent les sommets

avec sa voix d'insecte
et son visage de grand large

le geste illimité
l'écharpe serrée

le peigne est le dernier degré du geste
et je suis ce qui tombe
ce qui s'ajoute et ne s'ajoute plus
lieu du séjour et lieu du savoir

nommé
et aussitôt malgré moi
ressenti

dans le contre-jour de la mort

je me lève du fond de ma ressemblance
à la limite de l'énigme

soir après soir
j'ai disparu je disparais

elle s'éblouit
elle tombe dans le tissu du froid

parfois le retour
(est-ce la hâte)
soulage l'attardé

                    qui retarde au milieu de lui-même
la parole
pour figurer l'absence

le fil
tandis qu'il divulgue la fable de vie

parmi la trame imaginaire

l'autre révèle
le tisserand éternel

arc immense au-dessus de la mer
lorsque le dos plie
ou que le geste soulève l'avalanche
lorsque l'épaule cède

elle lisait quelque chose sur le saut quantique
elle lisait
        sans savoir
qu'elle achève ce que la lampe et la fenêtre commencent

parmi les trois lueurs

pure lampe de nul livre

loin
comme sembler

la voix blanche
quelle ligne contrainte pensive
allusive à ce qui n'est plus le toit le couloir

très pure

l'arbre efface l'eau et s'y recommence

j'entre et sors
et cherche ce qui s'ouvre et se referme

je vis s'évanouir sous le vent
la dernière lueur le dernier soir
dans le prolongement de la lumière

alors l'aile fut plus lente
et l'angle plus large

en travers du ciel
la tache déplia l'arbre l'eau

de l'autre côté
nulle feuille

rêvant la lente géométrie
de la dalle et de l'ardoise

tel théorème
à la découverte de ce qui est le toit le couloir

elle parle elle renouvelle ses précipices

elle dit
absente
elle était l'une des trois lueurs
à ne demeurer malgré le froid
éloignée de la fenêtre et de la lampe

elle dit
elle hanta ce que l'absence ne contient plus
la lueur
que lui étreignit avant elle
elle en éprouva un instant la douleur inconnue
d'innocenter la lampe et la fenêtre

.

Jean Daive (1941) is a French poet and translator living in Paris. He is the author of novels, collections of poetry and has translated work by Paul Celan and Robert Creeley among others. He has edited encyclopedias, worked as a radio journalist and producer with France Culture, and has edited four magazines: *fragment* (1969–72), *fig.* (1989–91), *FIN* (1999–2006) and *K.O.S.H.K.O.N.O.N.G.* (from 2013 to the present). Publishing since the 1960s, Daive is known as one of the important French avant-garde poets. Also a photographer, Daive chairs the Centre international de poésie de Marseille.

Norma Cole's books of poetry include *Win These Posters and Other Unrelated Prizes Inside*, *Where Shadows Will: Selected Poems 1988 – 2008*, *Spinoza in Her Youth* and *Natural Light*, and most recently *Actualities*, her collaboration with painter Marina Adams. *TO BE AT MUSIC: Essays & Talks* made its appearance in 2010 from Omnidawn. Her translations from the French include Danielle Collobert's *It Then*, Collobert's *Journals*, *Crosscut Universe: Writing on Writing from France* (edited and translated by Cole), and Jean Daive's *A Woman with Several Lives*. She lives in San Francisco.

White Decimal
by Jean Daive
translated by Norma Cole

Cover art by Ajit Chauhan: *Forty Miles Apart,*
typewriter ink, pencil on paper 11 3/4 x 8 1/4 inches.
Courtesy of the artist.

Cover and interior text set in Kabel LT Std and Garamond 3 LT Std
Cover and interior design by Gillian Olivia Blythe Hamel

Printed in the United States
by Edwards Brothers Malloy, Ann Arbor, Michigan
On 55# Glatfelter B18 Antique
Acid Free Archival Quality Recycled Paper

Publication of this book was made possible in part by gifts from:
The Clorox Company
The New Place Fund
Robin & Curt Caton

Omnidawn Publishing
Oakland, California
2017

Rusty Morrison & Ken Keegan, senior editors & co-publishers
Gillian Olivia Blythe Hamel, managing editor
Cassandra Smith, poetry editor & book designer
Sharon Zetter, poetry editor, book designer & development officer
Avren Keating, poetry editor, fiction editor & marketing assistant
Liza Flum, poetry editor
Juliana Paslay, fiction editor
Gail Aronson, fiction editor
Trisha Peck, marketing assistant
Cameron Stuart, marketing assistant
Natalia Cinco, marketing assistant
Maria Kosiyanenko, marketing assistant
Emma Thomason, administrative assistant
SD Sumner, copyeditor
Kevin Peters, *OmniVerse* Lit Scene editor
Sara Burant, *OmniVerse* reviews editor